This book belongs to

_____

The Classic
Mother Goose

THE CLASSIC MOTHER GOOSE

Edited by Armand Eisen

With illustrations by
John Gurney
Gail Nelson Hauetter
Arlene Klemushin
Kay Life
Robyn Officer
Richard Walz
Nancy Lee Wiley
William Arthur Wiley

COURAGE BOOKS

AN IMPRINT OF RUNNING PRESS
PHILADELPHIA • LONDON

10 9 8 7 6 5 4
Digit on the right indicates the number of this printing.

Library of Congress Cataloging-in-Publication Number
88-70839

ISBN 0-7624-0183-4

Designed by William Arthur Wiley
Art direction by Armand Eisen

Front cover illustration by Robyn Officer
Back cover, endpapers, front matter and
Illustrations on pages 13, 16, and 40 by William Arthur Wiley

Illustrations on pages 16, 17, 22, 23, 46, and 47 by John Gurney
Illustrations on pages 18, 19, 48, 49, 52, and 53 by Gail Nelson Hauetter
Illustrations on pages 26, 27, 36, and 37 by Arlene Klemushin
Illustrations on pages 28, 29, 38, 39, 41, 50, and 51 by Kay Life
Illustrations on pages 11, 20, 21, 24, 25, 34, 36, 42, 43, 44, 45, and 56
          by Robyn Officer
Illustrations on pages 12, 13, 30, and 31 by Richard Walz
Illustrations on pages 32, 33, 54, and 55 by Nancy Lee Wiley

Published by Courage Books, an imprint of
Running Press Book Publishers
125 South Twenty-second Street
Philadelphia, Pennsylvania 19103-4399

Foreword

There is hardly a child in the English-speaking world who does not know at least one or two Mother Goose rhymes.

When we were babies, unable to speak or understand the meaning of words, our parents sang the rhymes to us. By nursery school we began to learn the verses of Mother Goose by heart, making them our own. We recited the poems over and over again taking delight in the music of rhyme and meter, and discovering for the first time that our language can be fun and beautiful as well as a way of communicating.

Now grown-up and with children of our own, we re-experience the joy of the poems by teaching them to our sons and daughters. Thus, from one generation to the next, the charm, silliness and whimsey of Mother Goose is shared and passed down.

Mother Goose said it well when she rhymed,
"No, no, my melodies will never die,
While nurses sing and babies cry."

Armand Eisen
Editor

Contents

Baa, Baa, Black Sheep 27

Curly Locks! Curly Locks! 15

For Want Of A Nail 48

Handy Spandy 52

Hector Protector 53

Here We Go Round The Mulberry Bush 36

Hey Diddle Diddle 42

Hickory Dickory Dock 18

Humpty Dumpty 14

If Wishes Were Horses 49

Jack And Jill 17

Jack Be Nimble 19

Jack Sprat 47

Little Bo-Peep 20

Little Boy Blue 21

Little Jack Horner 52

Little King Boggen 40

Little Miss Muffet 29

Mary Had A Little Lamb 55

Mistress Mary, Quite Contrary 28

Oh, The Brave Old Duke Of York 51

Old King Cole 56

Old Mother Goose 11

Old Mother Hubbard 24

Pat-A-Cake 33

Pease Porridge Hot 33

Peter, Peter, Pumpkin Eater 16

Peter Piper 27

Polly, Put The Kettle On 50

Punch And Judy 41

Pussy Cat, Pussy Cat 13

Ride A Cock-Horse 49

Rock-A-Bye Baby 39

Rub-A-Dub-Dub 46

Simple Simon 32

Sing A Song of Sixpence 23

Sleep, Baby, Sleep. 38

Star Light, Star Bright. 34

The Lion And The Unicorn 22

The Man In The Moon. 34

The Queen Of Hearts. 12

There Was A Crooked Man 30

There Was An Old Woman 31

This Is The House That Jack Built 43

This Little Piggy 26

Three Blind Mice 19

Three Wise Men. 46

To Market, To Market. 37

Tom, Tom, the Piper's Son 54

Tweedledum and Tweedledee 12

Twinkle, Twinkle 35

Wee Willie Winkie 35

OLD MOTHER GOOSE, when
She wanted to wander,
Would ride through the air
On a very fine gander.

THE QUEEN OF HEARTS
She made some tarts,
All on a summer's day.
The Knave of Hearts
He stole the tarts,
And took them clean away.
The King of Hearts
Called for the tarts,
And beat the Knave full sore.
The Knave of Hearts
Brought back the tarts,
And vowed he'd steal no more.

TWEEDLEDUM AND TWEEDLEDEE
Agreed to fight a battle,
For Tweedledum said Tweedledee
Had spoiled his nice new rattle.
Just then flew by a monstrous crow,
As black as a tar-barrel,
Which frightened both the heroes so,
They quite forgot their quarrel.

PUSSY CAT, PUSSY CAT, where have you been?
I've been to London to look at the queen.
Pussy cat, pussy cat, what did you there?
I frightened a little mouse under her chair.

13

Humpty Dumpty sat on a wall,
    Humpty Dumpty had a great fall.
        All the king's horses and all the king's men,

Couldn't put Humpty Dumpty together again.

CURLY LOCKS! CURLY LOCKS! Wilt thou be mine?
Thou shalt not wash dishes, nor yet feed the swine;
But sit on a cushion and sew a fine seam,
And feed upon strawberries, sugar and cream!

PETER, PETER, PUMPKIN EATER,
Had a wife and couldn't keep her;
He put her in a pumpkin shell,
And there he kept her very well.

Peter, Peter, pumpkin eater,
Had another, and didn't love her;
Peter learned to read and spell,
And then he loved her very well.

JACK AND JILL went up the hill,
To fetch a pail of water;
Jack fell down and broke his crown,
And Jill came tumbling after.

Up Jack got, and home did trot,
As fast as he could caper,
To old Dame Dob, who patched his nob,
With vinegar and brown paper.

When Jill came in, how she did grin,
To see Jack's paper plaster;
Dame Dob, vexed, did whip her next
For laughing at Jack's disaster.

HICKORY, DICKORY, DOCK,
The mouse ran up the clock.
The clock struck one,
The mouse ran down,
And hickory, dickory, dock.

JACK BE NIMBLE,
Jack be quick,
Jack jump over the candlestick.

THREE BLIND MICE, see how they run!
They all ran after the farmer's wife,
Who cut off their tails with a carving knife.
Did you ever see such a sight in your life,
As three blind mice?

LITTLE BO-PEEP has lost her sheep,
And doesn't know where to find them.
Leave them alone, and they'll come home,
Dragging their tails behind them.

Little Bo-Peep fell fast asleep,
And dreamt she heard them bleating.
But when she awoke, she found it a joke,
For they were still a-fleeting.

Then up she took her little crook,
Determined for to find them;
She found them indeed,
But it made her heart bleed,
For they'd left all their tails behind them.

It happened one day,
As Bo-Peep did stray,
Into a meadow hard by,
That she espied their tails side by side,
All hung on a tree to dry.

She heaved a sigh, and wiped her eye,
And over hills and dale-o,
And tried what she could, as a shepherdess should,
To tack each again to its tail-o.

LITTLE BOY BLUE, come blow your horn,
The sheep's in the meadow, the cow's in the corn.
But where is the little boy who looks after the sheep?
He's under the haystack fast asleep.
Will you wake him? No, not I,
For if I do, he's sure to cry.

THE LION AND THE UNICORN
Were fighting for the crown;
The lion beat the unicorn,
All about the town.

Some gave them white bread,
And some gave them brown.
Some gave them plum cake
And drummed them out of town.

SING A SONG OF SIXPENCE,
A pocket full of rye,
Four and twenty blackbirds
Baked in a pie.

When the pie was opened,
The birds began to sing;
Was not that a dainty dish,
To set before the king?

The king was in his counting-house,
Counting out his money;
The queen was in the parlor,
Eating bread and honey,

The maid was in the garden,
Hanging out the clothes,
When along came a blackbird,
And snapped off her nose.
Along came a Jenny Wren
And popped it on again.

OLD MOTHER HUBBARD
Went to the cupboard
To fetch her poor dog a bone,
But when she got there
The cupboard was bare
And so the poor dog had none.

She went to the baker's
To buy him some bread,
But when she came back
The poor dog was dead.

She went to the undertaker's
To buy him a coffin,
But when she came back
The poor dog was laughing.

She took a clean dish
To get him some tripe,
But when she came back
He was smoking a pipe.

She went to the alehouse
To get him some beer,
But when she came back
The dog sat in a chair.

She went to the tavern
For white wine and red,
But when she came back
The dog stood on his head.

She went to the fruiterer's
To buy him some fruit,
But when she came back
He was playing the flute.

She went to the tailor's
To buy him a coat,
But when she came back
He was riding a goat.

She went to the hatter's
To buy him a hat,
But when she came back
He was feeding the cat.

She went to the barber's
To buy him a wig,
But when she came back
He was dancing a jig.

She went to the cobbler's
To buy him some shoes,
But when she came back
He was reading the news.

She went to the seamstress
To buy him some linen,
But when she came back
The dog was a-spinning.

She went to the hosier's
To buy him some hose,
But when she came back
He was dressed in his clothes.

The dame made a curtsey,
The dog made a bow,
The dame said, Your servant.
The dog said, Bow-wow.

THIS LITTLE PIGGY went to market,

This little piggy stayed home;

This little piggy had roast beef,

This little piggy had none,

And this little piggy cried wee-wee-wee all the way home.

BAA, BAA, BLACK SHEEP,
Have you any wool?
Yes sir, yes sir,
Three bags full:
One for my master,
One for my dame,
One for the little boy
Who lives down the lane.

PETER PIPER picked
A peck of pickled pepper
A peck of pickled pepper
Peter Piper picked.
If Peter Piper picked
A peck of pickled pepper,
Where's the peck of pickled pepper
Peter Piper picked?

MISTRESS MARY, QUITE CONTRARY,

How does your garden grow?
With silver bells, and cockle shells,
And pretty maids all in a row.

LITTLE MISS MUFFET
Sat on a tuffet,
Eating her curds and whey;
Along came a spider
Who sat down beside her
And frightened Miss Muffet away.

THERE WAS A CROOKED MAN,
And he walked a crooked mile,
He found a crooked sixpence
Against a crooked stile;
He bought a crooked cat,
Which caught a crooked mouse,
And they all lived together
In a little crooked house.

THERE WAS AN OLD WOMAN,
Who lived in a shoe,
She had so many children,
She didn't know what to do;
She gave them some broth,
Without any bread;
She whipped them all soundly,
And put them to bed.

SIMPLE SIMON met a pieman,
Going to the fair;
Says Simple Simon to the pieman,
Let me taste your ware.

Says the pieman to Simple Simon,
Show me first your penny.
Says Simple Simon to the pieman,
Indeed I have not any.

Simple Simon went a-fishing,
For to catch a whale;
All the water he had got
Was in his mother's pail.

Simple Simon went to look
If plums grew on a thistle;
He pricked his finger very much,
Which made poor Simon whistle.

PAT-A-CAKE, pat-a-cake, baker's man,
Bake me a cake as fast as you can.
Pat it and prick it,
And mark it with a T,
Put it in the oven for Tommy and me.

PEASE PORRIDGE HOT,
Pease porridge cold,
Pease porridge in the pot,
Nine days old.

Some like it hot,
Some like it cold,
Some like it in the pot,
Nine days old.

THE MAN IN THE MOON looked out of the moon,
Looked out of the moon and said,
" 'Tis time for all children on the earth,
To think about getting to bed!"

STAR LIGHT, STAR BRIGHT,
First star I see tonight,
I wish I may, I wish I might,
Have the wish I wish tonight.

TWINKLE, TWINKLE, little star,
How I wonder what you are!
Up above the world so high,
Like a diamond in the sky.

WEE WILLIE WINKIE,
Runs through the town,
Upstairs and downstairs,
In his night gown;
Rapping at the window,
Crying through the lock,
Are the children in their beds?
For now it's ten o'clock.

HERE WE GO ROUND THE MULBERRY BUSH,
The mulberry bush, the mulberry bush.
Here we go round the mulberry bush,
On a cold and frosty morning.

This is the way we wash our clothes,
Wash our clothes, wash our clothes.
This is the way we wash our clothes,
On a cold and frosty morning.

This is the way we clean our rooms,
Clean our rooms, clean our rooms.
This is the way we clean our rooms,
On a cold and frosty morning.

To MARKET, TO MARKET, to buy a fat pig,
Home again, home again, jiggety-jig;
To market, to market, to buy a fat hog,
Home again, home again, jiggety-jog.

SLEEP, BABY, SLEEP,
Thy father guards the sheep;
Thy mother shakes the dreamland tree,
And from it fall sweet dreams for thee.
Sleep, baby, sleep.

Sleep, baby, sleep,
Our cottage vale is deep;
The little lamb is on the green,
With woolly fleece so soft and clean,
Sleep, baby, sleep.

Sleep, baby, sleep,
Down where the woodbines creep;
Be always like the lamb so mild,
A kind and sweet and gentle child,
Sleep, baby, sleep.

ROCK-A-BYE BABY
On the tree top,
When the wind blows
The cradle will rock;
When the bough breaks
The cradle will fall;
Down will come baby,
Cradle and all.

LITTLE KING BOGGEN he built a fine hall,
Pie-crust and pastry crust, that was the wall,
The windows were made of black pudding and white,
And slated with pancakes—you ne'er saw the like.

PUNCH AND JUDY,
Fought for a pie,
Punch gave Judy
A sad blow in the eye.

Says Punch to Judy,
Will you have more?
Says Judy to Punch,
My eye is sore.

HEY DIDDLE, DIDDLE,
The cat and the fiddle,
The cow jumped over the moon;
The little dog laughed
To see such sport
And the dish ran away
with the spoon.

THIS IS THE HOUSE that Jack built.
This is the malt
That lay in the house that Jack built.

This is the rat,
That ate the malt
That lay in the house that Jack built.

This is the cat,
That killed the rat,
That ate the malt
That lay in the house that Jack built.

This is the dog,
That worried the cat,
That killed the rat,
That ate the malt
That lay in the house that Jack built.

This is the cow with the crumpled horn,
That tossed the dog,
That worried the cat,
That killed the rat,
That ate the malt
That lay in the house that Jack built.

This is the maiden all forlorn,
That milked the cow with the crumpled horn,
That tossed the dog,
That worried the cat,
That killed the rat,
That ate the malt
That lay in the house that Jack built.

This is the man all tattered and torn,
That kissed the maiden all forlorn,
That milked the cow with the crumpled horn,
That tossed the dog,
That worried the cat,
That killed the rat,
That ate the malt
That lay in the house that Jack built.

This is the priest all shaven and shorn,
That married the man all tattered and torn,
That kissed the maiden all forlorn,
That milked the cow with the crumpled horn,
That tossed the dog,
That worried the cat,
That killed the rat,
That ate the malt
That lay in the house that Jack built.

This is the cock that crowed in the morn,
That waked the priest all shaven and shorn,
That married the man all tattered and torn,
That kissed the maiden all forlorn,
That milked the cow with the crumpled horn,
That tossed the dog,
That worried the cat,
That killed the rat,
That ate the malt,
That lay in the house that Jack built.

This is the farmer sowing his corn,
That kept the cock that crowed in the morn,
That waked the priest all shaven and shorn,
That married the man all tattered and torn,
That kissed the maiden all forlorn,
That milked the cow with the crumpled horn,
That tossed the dog,
That worried the cat,
That killed the rat,
That ate the malt
That lay in the house that Jack built.

THREE WISE MEN of Gotham,
They went to sea in a bowl.
And if the bowl had been stronger,
My song had been longer.

RUB-A-DUB-DUB,
Three men in a tub,
And who do you think they be?
The butcher, the baker,
The candlestick-maker,
Turn 'em out,
Knaves all three!

JACK SPRAT could eat no fat,
His wife could eat no lean;
And so, betwixt them both, you see,
They licked the platter clean.

FOR WANT OF A NAIL the shoe was lost,
For want of a shoe the horse was lost,
For want of a horse the rider was lost,
For want of a rider the battle was lost,
For want of a battle the kingdom was lost,
And all for the want of a horseshoe nail.

IF WISHES WERE HORSES
Beggars would ride;
If turnips were watches
I would wear one by my side.
And if "ifs" and "ands" were pots and pans,
There'd be no work for tinkers!

RIDE A COCK-HORSE to Banbury Cross,
To see a fine lady upon a white horse;
Rings on her fingers and bells on her toes,
And she shall have music wherever she goes.

POLLY, PUT THE KETTLE ON,
Polly, put the kettle on,
Polly put the kettle on,
And let's drink tea.

Sukey take it off again,
Sukey take it off again,
Sukey take it off again,
They've all gone away.

OH, THE BRAVE OLD DUKE OF YORK,
He had ten thousand men;
He marched them up to the top of the hill,
And he marched them down again.
And when they were up, they were up,
And when they were down, they were down,
And when they were only half-way up,
They were neither up nor down.

LITTLE JACK HORNER
Sat in a corner,
Eating a Christmas pie;
He put in his thumb,
And pulled out a plum,
And said, what a good boy am I.

HANDY SPANDY, Jack a-dandy
Loves plum cake and sugar candy;
He bought some at a grocer's shop,
And out he came, hop-hop-hop.

HECTOR PROTECTOR was dressed all in green;
Hector Protector was sent to the Queen,
The Queen did not like him,
No more did the King.
So Hector Protector was sent back again.

Tom, tom, the piper's son,
Stole a pig and away did run;
The pig was eat, and Tom was beat,
And Tom ran crying down the street.

MARY HAD A LITTLE LAMB,
Its fleece was white as snow;
And everywhere that Mary went,
The lamb was sure to go.

It followed her to school one day,
That was against the rule;
It made the children laugh and play,
To see a lamb in school.

And so the teacher turned it out,
But still it lingered near,
And waited patiently about,
Till Mary did appear.

Why does the lamb love Mary so?
The eager children cry.
Why, Mary loves the lamb, you know,
The teacher did reply.

OLD KING COLE
Was a merry old soul,
And a merry old soul was he;
He called for his pipe,
And he called for his bowl,
And he called for his fiddlers three.

Every fiddler, he had a fiddle,
And a very fine fiddle had he;
Twee tweedle dee, tweedle dee, went the fiddlers.
Oh, there's none so rare
As can compare
With King Cole and his fiddlers three.